JAN. 06

Extent, Nature, and Consequences of Rape Victimization: Findings From the National Violence Against Women Survey

Patricia Tjaden and Nancy Thoennes

NCJ 210346

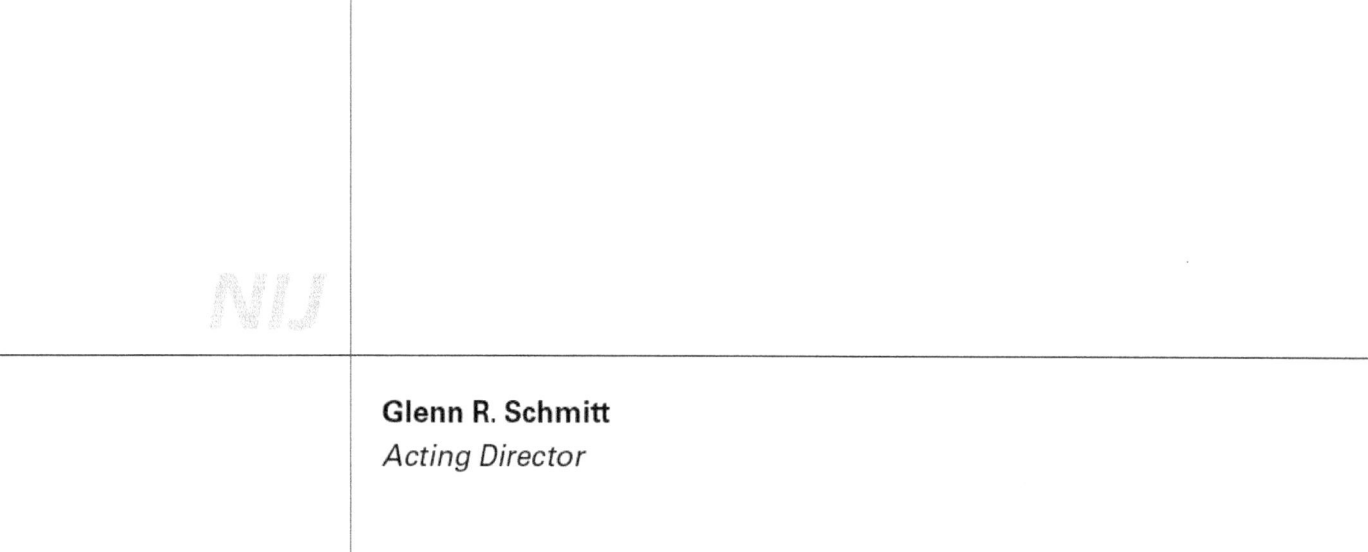

Glenn R. Schmitt
Acting Director

Findings and conclusions of the research reported here are those of the author(s) and do not necessarily reflect the official position or policies of the U.S. Department of Justice.

This research was sponsored by the U.S. Department of Justice, National Institute of Justice and the Centers for Disease Control and Prevention, under NIJ grant number 93–IJ–CX–0012.

The National Institute of Justice is a component of the Office of Justice Programs, which also includes the Bureau of Justice Assistance, the Bureau of Justice Statistics, the Office of Juvenile Justice and Delinquency Prevention, and the Office for Victims of Crime.

About This Report

In 1995 and 1996, the National Violence Against Women Survey (NVAWS) was conducted to measure the extent of violence against women. This nationally representative telephone survey asked 8,000 women and 8,000 men about their experiences as rape victims.

Despite an increase in research on rape in the past 30 years, gaps remain in the understanding of rape victimization. The survey elicited information on the prevalence of rape victimization by gender, age, and race/ethnicity; characteristics of rape victims, rapists, and rape incidents; the relationship between rape victimization as a minor and as an adult; physical, social, and psychological consequences of rape victimization; and satisfaction with the justice system.

What did the researchers find?

Almost 18 million women and almost 3 million men in the United States have been raped. One of every six women has been raped at some time. In a single year, more than 300,000 women and almost 93,000 men are estimated to have been raped. Rape prevalence rates were the same for minority and nonminority women, but differences were found by specific racial and ethnic group. Younger women were significantly more likely to report being raped at some time in their lives than older women. More than half of the female victims and nearly three-quarters of the male victims were raped before their 18th birthday. Women who reported being raped as minors were twice as likely to report being raped as adults.

Although the word "rape" is gender neutral, most rape victims are female (almost 86

percent), and most rapists are male. Female victims are significantly more likely than male victims to be raped by a current or former intimate partner and to sustain an injury during a rape. Many rape victims suffer serious mental health consequences. Only one in five adult women report their rape to the police. About half of the women raped as adults who had contact with police and about half who had contact with the courts were satisfied with their treatment.

What were the study's limitations?

Because only 24 women and 8 men reported during their interviews that they had been raped in the 12 months preceding the survey, the annual estimates should be viewed with caution. NVAWS most likely underestimates the actual number of annual rapes because it excludes rapes of children and adolescents and those who are homeless or live in institutions, group facilities, or residences without telephones. Because of the small number of Asian/Pacific Islander women identified by the survey who had been raped and the small number of men identified for several indicators (e.g., several race/ethnicity categories, relationship between early and subsequent rape victimization, injuries sustained during a rape), NVAWS could not develop reliable rape prevalence estimates or conduct statistical tests.

Who should read this study?

Criminal justice and public health researchers and practitioners; legislators, policymakers, and intervention planners at all levels of government.

Contents

Introduction

Rape is a significant social and health problem in the United States. Results from the National Violence Against Women Survey (NVAWS) revealed that 17.7 million women and 2.8 million men in the United States were forcibly raped at some time in their lives, with 302,091 women and 92,748 men forcibly raped in the year preceding the survey. NVAWS found that lifetime rape prevalence varies significantly by race and ethnicity. American Indian/Alaska Native women reported significantly higher rates of rape victimization over their lifetime than did women from all other racial and ethnic backgrounds (except Asian/Pacific Islander, of whom too few victims were in the study to reliably estimate rape prevalence). Mixed-race women reported significantly higher rates of rape victimization over their lifetimes than did Hispanic women and slightly higher rates than non-Hispanic white and African-American women.

About the Authors

Patricia Tjaden, Ph.D., is Director of Tjaden Research Corporation. Nancy Thoennes, Ph.D., is Associate Director of the Center for Policy Research.

Information from NVAWS confirms previous reports that rape occurs at an early age for many rape victims. More than 50 percent of the female victims and 70 percent of the male victims said they were raped before their 18th birthday. These findings are noteworthy because women who were raped before age 18 were twice as likely to report being raped as adults. Given these findings, it is evident that rape prevention strategies should focus on rapes committed against minors as well as adults.

Although rape is a gender-neutral crime, the NVAWS findings indicate that most rape victims are women and most rapists are men. They also show that victim-perpetrator relationship patterns varied across the lifespan for women but not for men. Women who were raped as children (before age 12) tended to be victimized by relatives; as adolescents (between ages 12 and 17) women tended to be raped by intimate partners and acquaintances; and as adults (after their 18th birthday) women tended to be raped by intimate partners. In comparison, male victims tended to be raped by acquaintances regardless of their age at the time of victimization.

The survey also produced compelling evidence of the physical, social, and psychological consequences of rape victimization. About 32 percent of the women and 16 percent of the men were injured during their most recent rape as an adult. Of the women who were injured, more than 35 percent received medical treatment. In addition, 33 percent of the women and almost 25 percent of the men raped as adults received counseling from a mental health professional as a result of their most recent rape. Almost 20 percent of the women and 10 percent of the men said they lost time from work.

Despite a steep increase in rape research and public education in the past 30 years, rape continues to be largely underreported. Only one in five women who were

raped as adults reported their rape to the police. Fear of their rapist, embarrassment, and not considering their rape a crime or police matter were the primary reasons women chose not to report their victimization to the police.

These findings underscore the need for law enforcement agencies and victim service providers to expand their services to rape victims and do more to convince them that reporting their rape to the police is worthwhile and appropriate.

What Is the National Violence Against Women Survey?

Many gaps in knowledge about rape victimization remain.[1] Estimates of the prevalence and incidence of rape vary widely from study to study.[2] Information about minority women's experiences with rape victimization is limited,[3] as is information about men's experiences as rape victims. Information on the social, physical, and psychological consequences of rape victimization also is insufficient.[4]

To help deepen understanding of rape as well as the broader issue of violence against women, the National Institute of Justice (NIJ) and the Centers for Disease Control and Prevention (CDC) jointly

sponsored—through a grant to the Center for Policy Research—a national telephone survey on violence against women conducted in 1995–96. Respondents to the National Violence Against Women Survey (NVAWS) were queried about their experiences as victims of various forms of violence, including rape. (See "Definitions and Survey Questions.") To provide a context for understanding women's experiences, the survey sampled both women and men. Thus, the survey provides comparable data on women's and men's experiences as rape victims (see "Survey Methodology").

DEFINITIONS AND SURVEY QUESTIONS

In the National Violence Against Women Survey (NVAWS), rape was defined as an event that occurred without the victim's consent that involved the use or threat of force in vaginal, anal, or oral intercourse. This definition closely resembles that used in the National Women's Study (NWS).[a] However, unlike NWS, NVAWS includes both attempted and completed rape. Thus, unless otherwise noted in this report, "rape" refers to both attempted and completed rape.

The survey included five behaviorally specific questions to screen for rape victimization. The first four questions are identical to those used in NWS and respectively screen for forced vaginal, oral, or anal penetration.[b] To collect information about attempted rape, NVAWS included a fifth question that screened for attempted forced penetration of the vagina, mouth, or anus. To minimize doubt in the respondent's mind about what

was being measured, the questions incorporated explicit language. (See "Rape Screening Questions," page 10.)

Respondents who replied "yes" to one or more of the screening questions were asked whether their rapist was a spouse, ex-spouse, male cohabiting partner, female cohabiting partner, relative, someone else they knew, or a stranger. To further delineate the victim-perpetrator relationship, interviewers asked respondents who disclosed rape victimization to specify which spouse/partner raped them (e.g., first ex-husband, current male cohabiting partner); or which relative raped them (e.g., father, brother, grandfather, mother, sister, aunt); or, in cases involving acquaintances, to specify the relationship they had with the rapist (e.g., date, boyfriend, girlfriend, boss, coworker, teacher, neighbor).

Continued on page 4

DEFINITIONS AND SURVEY QUESTIONS (cont.)

Respondents who disclosed rape were asked detailed questions about the characteristics and consequences of their rape, including the following:

- Where the rape occurred.

- Whether they or their rapist were using drugs or alcohol at the time of the incident.

- Whether their rapist used a gun, knife, or other weapon.

- Whether their rapist verbally threatened them.

- Whether their rapist physically assaulted them.

- Whether they thought they or someone close to them would be seriously harmed or killed by their rapist.

- Whether they were physically injured and, if so, the types of injuries incurred.

- Whether they received medical services.

- Whether they received counseling from a mental health professional.

- Whether they lost time from routine activities such as school, work, volunteer endeavors, recreational activities, and household chores.

- Whether they reported their rape to the police.

- Whether they obtained a restraining order against their rapist and, if so, whether it was violated.

- Whether their rapist was criminally prosecuted.

These questions were posed for each type of offender (e.g., spouse, ex-spouse, boyfriend, grandfather) identified by the victim. Victims who were raped more than once by the same type of offender were asked to use their *most recent rape* as a reference point.

NVAWS generated information on both the prevalence and incidence of rape. *Prevalence* refers to the number of people within a demographic group (e.g., women or men) who are victimized during a specific time period, such as the person's lifetime or the previous 12 months. *Incidence* refers to the number of separate victimizations, or incidents, perpetrated against people within a demographic group during a specific time period. Incidence expressed as a victimization rate is obtained by dividing the number of victimizations perpetrated against people in the demographic group by the number of people in the group and setting the rate to a standard population base, such as 1,000 people.[c]

Notes

a. National Victim Center and Crime Victims Research and Treatment Center, *Rape in America: A Report to the Nation,* Arlington, VA: National Victim Center and Charleston, SC: Crime Victims Research and Treatment Center, 1992.

b. Ibid.

c. Koss, M.P., and M.R. Harvey, *The Rape Victim: Clinical and Community Interventions,* 2d ed., Newbury Park, CA: Sage Publications, 1991.

This report summarizes findings from NVAWS on the extent, nature, and consequences of rape victimization among women and men in the United States. Information is presented on the following topics:

- Prevalence and incidence of rape victimization among women and men.

- Prevalence of rape victimization among minority populations.

- Prevalence of rape victimization among women and men in different age groups.

- Relationship between rape victimization at an early age and subsequent rape victimization.

- Characteristics of rape victims, rapists, and rape incidents.

- Frequency of injuries and sexually transmitted diseases incurred by adult victims.

■ Injured victims' use of medical services.

■ Frequency with which adult victims receive counseling from a mental health professional.

■ Frequency with which adult victims lose time from routine activities, such as work and school.

■ Adult victims' involvement and satisfaction with the justice system.

Survey Methodology

The National Violence Against Women Survey (NVAWS) was conducted from November 1995 to May 1996 by interviewers at Schulman, Ronca, Bucuvalas, Inc. (SRBI) under the direction of John Boyle.[a] The authors of this Special Report designed the survey questionnaire and conducted the analysis.[b]

The sample was drawn by random-digit dialing of households with a telephone in the 50 States and the District of Columbia. The sample was administered by U.S. Census region. Within each region, a simple random sample of working residential "hundreds banks" of phone numbers was drawn. (A hundreds bank is the first 8 digits of any 10-digit telephone number.) A randomly generated 2-digit number was appended to each randomly sampled hundreds bank to produce the full 10-digit, random-digit number. Separate banks of numbers were generated for male and female respondents. These random-digit numbers were called by SRBI interviewers from their central telephone facility, where nonworking and nonresidential numbers were screened out. When a residential household was reached, eligible adults were identified. In households with more than one eligible adult, the adult with the most recent birthday was selected as the designated respondent.

A total of 8,000 women and 8,005 men age 18 and older were interviewed using a computer-assisted telephone interviewing (CATI) system.

This report is one of a series on NVAWS published jointly by NIJ and CDC. Previous reports have focused on women's and men's experiences as victims of stalking, intimate partner violence, and violence in general. (See "Other Publications From the National Violence Against Women Survey" at the end of this report.)

(Five completed interviews with men were subsequently eliminated from the sample during data editing because of an excessive amount of inconsistent and missing data.) Only female interviewers surveyed female respondents. To test for possible bias introduced by the gender of the interviewer, a split-sample approach was used in the male sample whereby half of the interviews were conducted by female interviewers and half by male interviewers. A Spanish-language translation was administered by bilingual interviewers to Spanish-speaking respondents.

Because of the large number of interviews to be conducted, the survey was fielded as a series of replicate samples, with each replicate sample consisting of approximately 500–3,000 completed interviews. Replicate samples were generated using the same sample frame and sample design and, unless otherwise noted, were analyzed as one sample.

Two different sets of rape screening questions were fielded respectively during the first two female replicate samples to ascertain whether increasing the number of screening questions increases disclosure of rape victimization. Respondents in the first female replicate sample ($n = 500$) were asked two questions that respectively screened for attempted and completed forced penetration of the vagina, anus, or mouth

Continued on page 6

SURVEY METHODOLOGY (cont.)

by penis, and attempted and completed forced penetration of the vagina or anus by fingers, tongue, or objects. Respondents in the second female replicate sample (*n* = 501) were asked four questions that respectively screened for attempted and completed forced penetration of the vagina, anus, or mouth by penis; attempted and completed forced penetration of the mouth by penis or the vagina or anus by tongue; attempted and completed forced penetration of the anus by penis; and attempted and completed forced penetration of the vagina or anus by fingers, tongue, or objects.

Survey records from the two replicate samples were analyzed immediately following completion of the interviews to determine whether one set of questions yielded higher disclosure rates. Results indicate that the two sets of questions yield similar victimization rates: 21.6 percent of the women in the first replicate sample and 20.6 percent of the women in the second replicate sample said they were the victim of an attempted and/or completed rape at some time in their lifetime. It should be noted that because both sets of screening questions combine questions about attempted and completed rape, it is impossible to estimate attempted rape and completed rape victimization rates using the corresponding 1,001 survey records.

Following the analysis, the survey questionnaire was modified to include five different rape screening questions. (See "Rape Screening Questions," p. 10.) The first four questions are identical to those used in the National Women's Study (NWS) and screen respectively for forced penile-vaginal penetration, forced penetration of the mouth by penis or the vagina or anus by tongue, forced penile-anal penetration, and forced penetration of the vagina or anus by fingers or objects.[c] The fifth question screens for

attempted forced penetration of the vagina, mouth, or anus. This version of the questionnaire was administered to the remaining 6,999 female respondents and all the male respondents (who were not queried about forced vaginal penetration). Because this version of the questionnaire replicates screening questions used in NWS, rape victimization estimates generated from the 6,999 survey records are directly comparable to rape victimization estimates generated from NWS. Moreover, because this version includes separate questions about attempted rape and completed rape, the survey records can be used to ascertain separate victimization rates for attempted rape and completed rape.

To determine the representativeness of the sample, select demographic characteristics of the NVAWS sample were compared with demographic characteristics of the general population from the U.S. Census Bureau's 1995 Current Population Survey of adult men and women.[d]

Notes

a. John Boyle, Ph.D., is senior partner and director of the Government and Social Research Division at SRBI. He specializes in public policy research in the area of health and violence and manages SRBI's Washington, D.C., office.

b. An indepth analysis of the statistical methodology can be found in *Full Report of the Prevalence, Incidence, and Consequences of Violence Against Women: Findings From the National Violence Against Women Survey* (see "Other Publications From the National Violence Against Women Survey," p. 40 of this report).

c. National Victim Center and Crime Victims Research and Treatment Center, *Rape in America: A Report to the Nation,* Arlington, VA: National Victim Center and Charleston, SC: Crime Victims Research and Treatment Center, 1992.

d. A technical report that describes the survey methods in more detail and records sample characteristics and prevalence rates using weighted and unweighted data is available from the Center for Policy Research, 1570 Emerson Street, Denver, CO 80218; phone: 303–837–1555; fax: 303–837–1557; e-mail: cntrpolres@qwest.net.

Prevalence and Incidence of Rape

Using a definition of rape that includes attempted and completed vaginal, oral, and anal penetration achieved through the use or threat of force, NVAWS found that 17.6 percent of surveyed women and 3 percent of surveyed men were raped at some time in their lives (see exhibit 1). Thus, in the United States, 1 of every 6 women has been raped at some time in her life, and 1 of every 33 men has been raped at some time in his life. Based on U.S. Census estimates of the number of women and men age 18 and older in the United States in 1995 (the year the sample was generated), 17.7 million women and 2.8 million men in the United States have been raped at some time in their life (see exhibit 1).

The study also found that 0.3 percent of surveyed women and 0.1 percent of surveyed men were raped in the 12 months preceding the survey. Based on 1995 census estimates of the number of women and men age 18 and older in the Nation, 302,091 women and 92,748 men were raped in 1995, a year that approximates the timeframe of the study.[5] Because some victims were raped more than once in the 12 months preceding the survey, the estimated number of rapes perpetrated in the United States in 1995 exceeds the estimated number of rape victims. Specifically, female victims averaged 2.9 rapes and male victims averaged 1.2 rapes in the 12 months preceding the survey. Thus, an estimated 876,064 rapes were

Exhibit 1. Percentage and number of women and men who were raped in lifetime and previous 12 months

Rape timeframe	Percentage		Number[a]	
	Women (*n* = 8,000)	Men (*n* = 8,000)	Women (100,697,000)	Men (92,748,000)
Raped in lifetime[b]	17.6	3.0	17,722,672	2,782,440
Raped in previous 12 months	0.3	0.1	302,091	92,748

a. Estimates are based on women and men age 18 and older. Wetrogan, S.I., *Projections of the Population of States by Age, Sex, and Race: 1988 to 2010,* Current Population Reports, Series P25–1017, Washington, DC: U.S. Bureau of the Census, 1988.

b. Difference between women and men is statistically significant.

Note: Lifetime prevalence rates for women in this exhibit are based on survey records of 6,999 women who were administered a version of the survey questionnaire that contains separate questions about attempted rape and completed rape. The remaining 1,001 women were administered versions of the questionnaire that combine questions about attempted rape and completed rape. Because it is impossible to distinguish attempted rape and completed rape from the combined questions, the corresponding 1,001 survey records were excluded when attempted rape and completed rape rates for women were calculated. The 1,001 survey records also were excluded when the total lifetime rape rate for women presented here was calculated to make this rate consistent with information in exhibit 3, which presents rape estimates for both lifetime attempted rape and lifetime completed rape. (See "Survey Methodology" for more information about different versions of the NVAWS questionnaire.)

committed against U.S. women and an estimated 111,298 rapes were perpetrated against U.S. men in 1995 (see exhibit 2). Because 1995 rape estimates are based on responses from only 24 women and 8 men who reported being raped in the 12 months preceding the survey, the data are unstable and should be viewed with caution. Annual estimates presented in this report also probably underestimate the true number of rapes committed each year because they exclude attempted/completed rapes of children and adolescents and attempted/completed rapes of women and men who are homeless or living in institutions (e.g., prisons, mental hospitals), group facilities (e.g., dormitories, halfway houses), or households without telephones.

Attempted rape versus completed rape

Interviewers queried respondents about their experiences as victims of both attempted and completed rape. Attempted rapes refer to incidents in which rapists threatened or used force to attempt vaginal, anal, or oral rape, but penetration did not occur. As shown in exhibit 3, relatively few women and men reported they were the victims of an attempted rape *only*. Among all respondents, 14.8 percent of the women and 2.1 percent of the men said they were victims of a completed rape at some time in their life, whereas 2.8 percent of the women and 0.9 percent of the men said they were victims of an attempted rape *only*. (Women and men

who said they were victims of a completed rape may also have been victims of an attempted rape.)

These findings are noteworthy for two reasons. They indicate that most rapists are successful in penetrating their victims. They also demonstrate how the definition of rape used in a research study affects who is counted as a victim and, consequently, victimization rates. Research will find higher rape victimization rates if studies include attempts in their definition of rape, illustrating the maxim that the broader the definition used to measure victimization, the higher the victimization rate.

Comparison with previous rape estimates

Lifetime estimates. Before NVAWS, national information on rape occurring over a victim's lifetime was limited to data from two nationwide studies on forced sex. The 1992 National Health and Social Life Survey (NHSLS) interviewed a national probability sample of U.S. women and men about their experiences with sex, including forced sex, and found that 22 percent of women and 2 percent of men had been "forced to do something sexual in their life."[6] The 1990 National Women's Study (NWS) surveyed a national probability sample of U.S. women about their experiences with completed but not attempted rape and found that 13 percent of women had been raped at some time in their lives.[7]

Exhibit 2. Number of rapes perpetrated against women and men in the previous 12 months

Victims' gender	Number of rape victims	Average number of rapes per victim	Total number of rapes	Rape rate per 1,000 women/men
Women	302,091	2.9	876,064	8.7
Men	92,748	1.2	111,298	1.2

The NVAWS estimates are not directly comparable to NHSLS estimates because the two surveys used different screening questions and measured somewhat different phenomena. Specifically, NVAWS used five questions to screen for attempted and completed rape; NHSLS used only one question to screen for "being forced to do something sexual." Nonetheless, NHSLS findings provide a context for NVAWS's lifetime rape prevalence estimates. NVAWS's estimate that 17.6 percent of women have been victims of an attempted/completed rape is lower than NHSLS's 22 percent estimate. In contrast, the NVAWS estimate that 3 percent of men have been victims of an attempted/completed rape is higher than NHSLS's 2 percent estimate. Although the two surveys generated different estimates for somewhat different phenomena, results from both surveys show that forced sex is a widespread problem in U.S. society, especially among women.

NVAWS and NWS were conducted in different years (1995–96 and 1990, respectively), but their estimates are comparable because they used identical screening questions for completed rape (see "Survey Methodology" and "Rape Screening Questions"). The NVAWS estimate that

14.8 percent of women have been victims of a completed rape (see exhibit 3) is slightly higher than the NWS estimate of 13 percent. Because of sampling errors associated with both surveys, the difference between the NVAWS and NWS estimates may be insignificant.

Annual estimates. The U.S. Department of Justice's Bureau of Justice Statistics (BJS) generates estimates about the number of attempted/completed rapes perpetrated against women and men in the United States annually using information generated from the National Crime Victimization Survey (NCVS). For 1995— a year that approximates the timeframe for NVAWS—NCVS estimates 214,783 attempted/completed rapes of females age 12 and older and 19,338 attempted/completed rapes of males age 12 and older.[8] NVAWS annual rape estimates are higher than those of NCVS, even though the NVAWS estimates include only attempted/completed rapes perpetrated against women and men age 18 and older. Specifically, the NVAWS estimate that 876,064 attempted/completed rapes were perpetrated against women age 18 and older in 1995 is four times greater than the 1995 NCVS estimate, and the NVAWS estimate of 111,298 attempted/completed

Exhibit 3. **Percentage of women and men who were victims of a completed versus attempted rape in lifetime**

Rape category	Women (%) (n = 8,000)	Men (%) (n = 8,000)
Raped in lifetime*	17.6	3.0
Completed rape*	14.8	2.1
Attempted rape only*	2.8	0.9

* Difference between women and men is statistically significant.

Note: Lifetime prevalence rates for women in this exhibit are based on survey records of 6,999 women who were administered a version of the survey questionnaire that contains separate questions about attempted and completed rape. The remaining 1,001 women were administered versions of the questionnaire that combine questions about attempted and completed rape. Because it is impossible to distinguish attempted rape and completed rape from the combined questions, the corresponding 1,001 survey records were excluded when attempted and completed rape rates for women were calculated. (See "Survey Methodology" for more information about different versions of the NVAWS questionnaire.)

rapes against men age 18 and older in 1995 is nearly six times greater than the 1995 NCVS estimate.

As noted in previous reports that summarize NVAWS findings,[9] direct comparisons between NVAWS and NCVS are difficult because estimates reported by the two surveys refer to somewhat different populations (individuals age 18 and older versus those 12 and older). Moreover, the two surveys' methodologies differ significantly, especially in terms of screening questions. NVAWS uses five questions to screen respondents for rape victimization (see "Rape Screening Questions"), while NCVS uses only two questions.[10] Although empirical data on this issue are limited, some researchers believe that increasing the number of screening questions increases victimization disclosure rates.[11] Furthermore, the NVAWS questions use more explicit language than those of NCVS.

In addition, NCVS estimates count series victimizations—reports of six or more crimes within a 6-month period for which the respondent cannot recall details of each crime—as a single victimization. Thus, NCVS estimates of the number of attempted/completed rapes are lower than would be obtained by including all incidents reported to its survey interviewers. To compare NCVS estimates directly with NVAWS estimates, NCVS would have to count each crime in a reported series of victimizations separately.

Rape prevalence compared with other forms of violence

What is the relative risk of being raped versus physically assaulted or stalked? NVAWS found that 1.9 percent of all surveyed women were physically assaulted in the 12 months preceding the survey, while 1 percent were stalked (see exhibit 4). Thus, in the year preceding the survey, U.S. women were six times more likely to be physically assaulted than raped and three times more likely to be stalked than

RAPE SCREENING QUESTIONS

The following questions screened respondents for completed and attempted rape victimization:*

■ *[Female respondents only]* Regardless of how long ago it happened, has a man or boy ever made you have sex by using force or threatening to harm you or someone close to you? Just so there is no mistake, by sex we mean putting a penis in your vagina.

■ Has anyone, male or female, ever made you have oral sex by using force or threat of force? Just so there is no mistake, by oral sex we mean that a man or boy put his penis in your mouth or someone, male or female, penetrated your vagina or anus with their mouth or tongue.

■ Has anyone ever made you have anal sex by using force or threat of harm? Just so there is no mistake, by anal sex we mean that a man or boy put his penis in your anus.

■ Has anyone, male or female, ever put fingers or objects in your vagina or anus against your will or by using force or threats?

■ Has anyone, male or female, ever *attempted* to make you have vaginal, oral, or anal sex against your will, but intercourse or penetration did not occur?

Note

* Rape screening questions were adapted from those used in the National Women's Study; see National Victim Center and Crime Victims Research and Treatment Center, *Rape in America: A Report to the Nation*, Arlington, VA: National Victim Center and Charleston, SC: Crime Victims Research and Treatment Center, 1992: 15.

raped. NVAWS also found that 3.4 percent of all surveyed men were physically assaulted in the 12 months preceding the survey, while 0.4 percent were stalked. Because so few men (*N* = 8) reported being raped in the previous 12 months, ratios of the likelihood of rape versus physical assault or stalking for men could not be completed.

Type of rape experienced

As the NVAWS screening questions show (see "Rape Screening Questions"), female respondents were asked specifically about different types of forced completed or attempted vaginal, oral, or anal penetration. Questions for men omitted reference to vaginal penetration. Exhibit 5 shows the types of rape female victims experienced, with 68.2 percent reporting forced penile-vaginal penetration. In addition, 49.3 percent of the women said they were victims of forced attempts to penetrate their vagina, anus, or mouth.

Among male victims, 52.7 percent said they experienced forced penetration of the mouth by penis or of the anus by tongue, 23.8 percent said they experienced forced penile-anal penetration, and 53.1 percent said they experienced attempted forced penetration of their anus or mouth.

Exhibit 4. **Percentage of women and men who were victimized in previous 12 months by type of violence**

	Victimized in previous 12 months	
Type of violence	Women (%) (*n* = 8,000)	Men (%) (*n* = 8,000)
Rape	0.3	0.1
Physical assault*	1.9	3.4
Stalking*	1.0	0.4

* Difference between women and men is statistically significant.

Exhibit 5. **Percentage distribution of female and male rape victims by type of rape experienced**

Type of rape experienced[a]	Female victims (%)[b] (*n* = 1,235)	Male victims (%)[b] (*n* = 239)
Penetration of vagina by penis	68.2	NA
Penetration of mouth by penis or vagina or anus by tongue	23.9	52.7
Penetration of anus by penis	13.4	23.8
Penetration of vagina or anus by objects or fingers	31.3	20.1
Attempted penetration of vagina, anus, or mouth	49.3	53.1

a. Questions to male respondents omitted reference to vaginal penetration.

b. Total percentages by victim gender exceed 100 because some victims experienced more than one type of rape.

Number of rapists

Most victims identified by the survey were raped by just one person over their lifetimes. Among female rape victims, 78.2 percent were raped by one person, 13.5 percent were raped by two people, and 8.3 percent were raped by three or more people (see exhibit 6). Among male rape victims, the comparable figures are 83.3 percent, 12.1 percent, and 4.6 percent, respectively. The survey found no statistically significant difference in the number of male and female victims raped by multiple rapists. It should be noted that victims who reported being raped by more than one person may have been raped by multiple people during a single incident, by different lone offenders during multiple incidents, or both.

Exhibit 6. **Percentage distribution of female and male victims by number of rapists in lifetime**

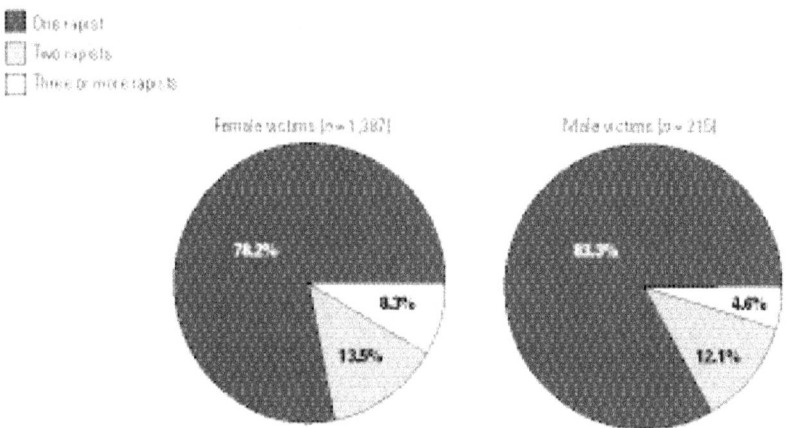

Rape Prevalence Among Minority Populations

To further understanding of the relationship between victimization and race/ethnicity, respondents were asked whether they would best classify themselves as white, black or African-American, Asian or Pacific Islander, American Indian or Alaska Native, mixed race, or of Hispanic origin. The response rate was extremely high—98 percent of the respondents answered the question about race, and 99 percent answered the question about Hispanic origin.

Combining data on Hispanic, African-American, American Indian/Alaska Native, Asian/Pacific Islander, and mixed-race women revealed no statistically significant difference in rape prevalence between minority and nonminority women—19 percent of minority women and 17.9 percent of non-Hispanic white women reported being raped at some time in their lifetime (see exhibit 7). Nor was a statistically significant difference in rape prevalence found between minority and nonminority men—3.4 percent of minority men reported being raped at some time in their lifetime compared with 2.8 percent of non-Hispanic white men.

However, comparisons of lifetime rape prevalence among women from specific racial/ethnic backgrounds showed some statistically significant differences. American Indian/Alaska Native women were significantly more likely than women from all other backgrounds to have been raped at some time in their lifetime (see exhibit 8), except for Asian/Pacific Islander women (of which too few victims were interviewed to reliably estimate rape prevalence or conduct statistical tests).

These findings are consistent with previous research showing that Native Americans experience more violence than other

Exhibit 7. Percentage of women and men who were raped in lifetime by minority status

Victims' gender	Minority (%)[a]	Nonminority (%)[b]
Women	19.0 (n = 1,633)	17.9 (n = 6,217)
Men	3.4 (n = 1,509)	2.8 (n = 6,250)

a. Minority includes respondents who self-identified as Hispanic white, African-American, Asian/Pacific Islander, American Indian/Alaska Native, or mixed race.

b. Nonminority includes respondents who self-identified as non-Hispanic white.

Note: Rates for women in this exhibit are based on 8,000 records of survey data and are higher than the rates for women presented in exhibits 1 and 3. Rates for women in exhibits 1 and 3 are based on the 6,999 survey records that correspond to the version of the survey questionnaire that contains separate questions about attempted rape and completed rape. This version of the questionnaire produced lower lifetime rates than those produced by versions that combine questions about attempted rape and completed rape.

Americans. A BJS study found that the rate of violent victimization among Native Americans was more than twice the rate for the Nation (124 versus 50 per 1,000 people ages 12 and older).[12] A study by the National Center for Injury Prevention and Control found that homicide rates for Native Americans were about twice that of national U.S. rates.[13] Another study that used data from the 1985 Family Violence Survey found that Native American couples were significantly more violent than their white counterparts.[14] How much of the variance between American Indian/Alaska Native women and women from other racial/ethnic backgrounds may be explained by demographic, social, and environmental factors remains unclear and requires further study. Moreover, significant differences in rape prevalence between American Indian and Alaska Native women may be found that cannot be discerned from this study because it combined information on the two groups. Significant intertribal differences within American Indian and Alaska Native groups also may exist.

The survey also found that Hispanic white women had significantly lower lifetime rape prevalence rates than mixed-race women. However, the difference in rape prevalence was not statistically significant between Hispanic white women and non-Hispanic white women. This finding contradicts conclusions from previous studies that compared sexual assault prevalence among mostly Mexican-American women and non-Hispanic white women.[15] The study also found no statistically significant difference among non-Hispanic white women, African-American women, or mixed-race women—17.9 percent of non-Hispanic white women, 18.8 percent of African-American women, and 24.4 percent of mixed-race women were raped at some time in their lives.

Unfortunately, the study could not develop reliable rape prevalence estimates or conduct statistical tests for Asian/Pacific Islander women because too few rape victims were identified from the survey. Research has suggested that intimate partner victimization rates are lower for Asian and Pacific Islander women than

Exhibit 8. Percentage of women and men who were raped in lifetime by race/ethnicity

Victims' gender	Non-Hispanic white (%)	Hispanic white (%)	African-American (%)	American Indian/ Alaska Native (%)	Mixed race (%)	Asian/Pacific Islander (%)
Women[a]	17.9 (n = 6,217)	11.9 (n = 235)	18.8 (n = 780)	34.1 (n = 88)	24.4 (n = 397)	6.8 (n = 133)
Men	2.8 (n = 6,250)	—[b] (n = 174)	3.3 (n = 659)	—[b] (n = 105)	4.4 (n = 406)	—[b] (n = 165)

a. Difference between Hispanic white and mixed-race women and between American Indian/Alaska Native and all other non-Asian/Pacific Islander women is statistically significant.

b. Estimates were not calculated on five or fewer victims.

Note: Rates for women in this exhibit are based on 8,000 records of survey data and are higher than the rates for women presented in exhibits 1 and 3. Rates for women in exhibits 1 and 3 are based on the 6,999 survey records that correspond to the version of the survey questionnaire that contains separate questions about attempted rape and completed rape. This version of the questionnaire produced lower lifetime rates than those produced by versions that combine questions about attempted rape and completed rape.

women of other minority backgrounds because traditional Asian values may discourage them from disclosing such victimization, even in confidential settings.[16] More research is needed to determine whether traditional values discourage Asian women from disclosing rape victimization or whether they actually experience less rape victimization than women from other racial/ethnic backgrounds.

NVAWS compared rape prevalence among men from different racial/ethnic backgrounds and found no statistically s i gnificant difference among African-American, mixed-race, and non-Hispanic white men. Too few Hispanic white, Asian/Pacific Islander, and American Indian/Alaska Native male victims were identified to reliably estimate rape prevalence or conduct statistical tests for these groups.

Rape Prevalence by Age

To provide information about rape prevalence and age, lifetime rape victimization rates were compared for women and men who were ages 18–29, 30–39, 40–49, 50–59, and 60 years and older at the time of the survey. Lifetime rape prevalence varied significantly by age group for women but not for men. About one-fifth of the women who were ages 18–29 (22.4 percent), 30–39 (21.8 percent), and 40–49 (21.2 percent) at the time of the survey said they were raped at some time in their life, compared with 16.6 percent of the women who were ages 50–59 and 6.9 percent who were age 60 and older (see exhibit 9). Thus, 1 in 5 women who were 18–49 years old at the time of the survey had been raped, compared with 1 in 6 women who were ages 50–59 and 1 in 15 women who were age 60 and older. The relatively low rape prevalence for women ages 50–59 and 60 and older is especially noteworthy given that women in these age groups were at risk for a longer time than younger women.

At first glance, these findings suggest that rape prevalence has increased over the past 50 years. However, it is also possible that younger women (i.e., women 18–49 years old) were simply more willing than older women to report their victimization to interviewers. Previous research has shown that older women who meet the legal definition of a crime victim are less likely than younger female crime victims to label themselves as such. For example, a study of wife rape found that older women who met the legal definition of being a marital rape victim were less likely to define themselves as such than younger women victimized this way.[17] Similarly, in a study comparing legal and victim definitions of stalking, NVAWS found that older women who met the legal definition of having been stalked were less likely than younger women who were also stalked to label themselves as stalking victims.[18] More research is needed to determine whether rape victimization has increased over time and, if so, what demographic,

Exhibit 9. **Percentage of women and men who were raped in lifetime by age at time of survey**

Victims' gender	Age in years (%)				
	18–29	30–39	40–49	50–59	60+
Women*	22.4 (n = 1,524)	21.8 (n = 1,934)	21.2 (n = 1,767)	16.6 (n = 1,131)	6.9 (n = 1,498)
Men	3.5 (n = 1,722)	3.6 (n = 2,008)	2.9 (n = 1,899)	2.1 (n = 1,067)	2.1 (n = 1,223)

* Difference between women age 50–59 and all other age groups and women age 60 and older and all other age groups is statistically significant.

social, economic, and environmental factors have led to this increase. Research is
also needed on the relationships among
age, victimization, and self-identification
as a victim.

Rape occurs at an early age

Survey results show that rape occurs at an
early age for many rape victims—21.6 percent of women and 48 percent of men
were younger than 12 years old when they
were first raped, and 32.4 percent of
women and 23 percent of men were
between ages 12 and 17. Thus, more than
half (54 percent) of female victims and
nearly three-quarters (71 percent) of male
victims were first raped before their 18th
birthday. In comparison, 29.4 percent of
female victims and 16.6 percent of male
victims were 18 to 24 years old when they
were first raped, and 16.6 percent of

female victims and 12.3 percent of male
victims were age 25 or older (see exhibit
10). These findings are consistent with
findings from the National Women's Study,
which shows that many U.S. women are
raped as children and adolescents.[19]

Although most rape victims identified by
NVAWS were under 18 when they were
first raped, the survey found that more
women were raped as adults than as children or adolescents. Among all women
surveyed, 9.6 percent said they were
raped as an adult, 6.3 percent said they
were raped as an adolescent, and 3.6 percent said they were raped as a child (see
exhibit 11). When the proportion of women
who were raped before and after their
18th birthday was compared, the study
found that women were nearly equally
likely to be raped as minors and adults.
Specifically, 9.1 percent of all women surveyed said they were raped before their

Exhibit 10. Percentage distribution of female and male rape victims by age at time of first rape

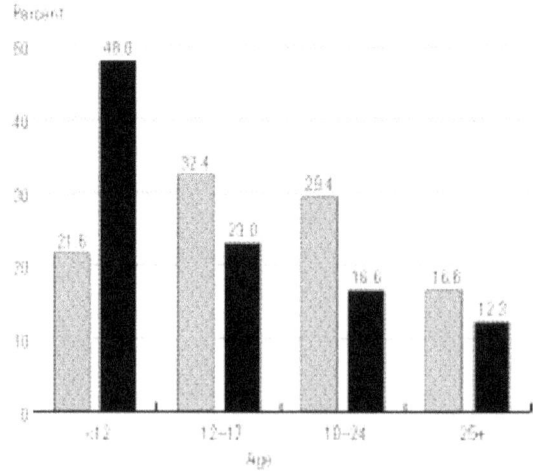

Note: Total percentage for male victims is less than 100 due to rounding.

18th birthday (not shown), while 9.6 percent said they were raped since they turned 18.

Rape prevalence patterns differ for men. Among all surveyed men, 1.3 percent said they were raped as a child, 0.7 percent said they were raped as an adolescent, and 0.8 percent said they were raped as an adult (see exhibit 11). Thus, men were nearly twice as likely to be raped as children than as adolescents or adults. It should be noted that for every age group considered (child, adolescent, and adult), women reported significantly more rapes than men. Because a respondent could have been raped as a child, adolescent, and/or adult, age categories are not mutually exclusive. Thus, the percentages of child, adolescent, and adult rape victims cannot be added to get the total percentage of rape victims.

Prevalence of early rape victimization by age

The study found that age at the time of the survey and being raped as a child and/or adolescent were inversely related for women. Specifically, 14.5 percent of the women who were 18 to 29 years old at the time of the survey said they were raped before their 18th birthday, compared with 11.8 percent of the women who were 30 to 39, 8.5 percent who were 40 to 59, 7 percent who were 50 to 59, and 2.6 percent who were age 60 or older (see exhibit 12). The difference in the rate of early rape victimization for women is statistically significant between all age groups except between women ages 40 to 49 and 50 to 59.

These findings suggest that the risk of being raped as a child or adolescent has increased steadily for women over the past half century. As previously noted, however, it is possible that younger women are simply more likely than older women to identify themselves as victims, including victims of child and adolescent rape, and more likely to report their victimization to an interviewer.

The relationship between age at the time of the survey and being raped as a child and/or adolescent is less clear for men. Although men who were 18 to 39 years old at the time of the survey were more likely to report being raped before their 18th birthday than men who were age 40 or older, the difference in the rate of early rape victimization is not statistically significant between any of the male age groups (see exhibit 12). Thus, it is impossible to conclude that the risk of being raped as a child or adolescent has increased for men over the past 50 years.

Exhibit 11. Percentage of women and men who were raped as a child, adolescent, and/or adult

Age category of victim[a,b]	Women (%) (n = 8,000)	Men (%) (n = 8,000)
Child (ages 0–11)	3.6	1.3
Adolescent (ages 12–17)	6.3	0.7
Adult (age 18 and older)	9.6	0.8

a. Difference between women and men is statistically significant.

b. Age categories are not mutually exclusive and therefore cannot be added to get the total percentage of victims.

Exhibit 12. **Percentage of women and men who were raped before age 18 by age at time of survey**

	Age in years (%)				
Victims' gender	18–29	30–39	40–49	50–59	60+
Women*	14.5 (n = 1,524)	11.8 (n = 1,934)	8.5 (n = 1,767)	7.0 (n = 1,131)	2.6 (n = 1,498)
Men	2.3 (n = 1,722)	2.3 (n = 2,008)	1.9 (n = 1,899)	1.3 (n = 1,067)	1.3 (n = 1,223)

* Difference between women in all groups except 40–49 and 50–59 is statistically significant.

Relationship between early and subsequent rape victimization

Previous research indicates that women who are sexually assaulted as children or adolescents are more likely to be sexually assaulted as adults.[20] Results from NVAWS are consistent with this research: 18.3 percent of the women who said they were raped before age 18 also reported being raped since their 18th birthday, compared with 8.7 percent of the women who did not report being raped before age 18. Thus, women who were raped as minors were twice as likely to report being raped as adults. (The number of male victims was insufficient to analyze the relationship between early and subsequent rape victimization for men.)

Although these findings establish a strong link between rape victimization as a minor and subsequent rape victimization as an adult, the link is not necessarily causal. Early rape victimization may possibly pose a genuine risk for subsequent rape victimization, but some other persistent risk factor, such as poverty or sexual orientation, could possibly lead to early and subsequent rape. The relationship between early and subsequent rape victimization reflected in NVAWS data also may simply reflect the fact that respondents who are willing to disclose to interviewers that they were raped as children or adolescents are also more willing to disclose that they were raped as adults. More research is needed on these issues. If early victimization poses a genuine risk for subsequent victimization, research is needed on effective intervention strategies to mitigate this risk.

Characteristics of Rape Victims, Rapists, and Rape Incidents

Victim and offender gender

Although rape is a gender-neutral crime, most rape victims are women and most rapists are men. Among all rape victims identified by the survey, 85.8 percent were women and 14.2 percent were men. Nearly all of the female victims (99.6 percent) and most of the male victims (85.2 percent) were raped by a male, while less than 1 percent of the female victims and 18.2 percent of the male victims were raped by a female. (Total percentages for male and female victims exceed 100, because some victims were raped by both a male and a female.)

Victim-offender relationship

Information from NVAWS confirms previous research that shows most rape victims know their rapist. Only 16.7 percent of all female victims and 22.8 percent of all male victims were raped by a stranger (see exhibit 13). In general, female victims tended to be raped by current or former intimates, defined in this study as spouses, male and female cohabiting partners, dates, boyfriends, and girlfriends. In comparison, male victims tended to be raped by acquaintances, such as friends, teachers, coworkers, or neighbors. Among all female victims identified by the survey, 20.2 percent were raped by a spouse or ex-spouse, 4.3 percent were raped by a current or former cohabiting partner, and 21.5 percent were raped by a current or former date, boyfriend, or girlfriend. Among all male victims, 4.1 percent were

raped by a spouse or ex-spouse, 3.7 percent were raped by a current or former cohabiting partner, and 2.7 percent were raped by a current or former date, boyfriend, or girlfriend.

Overall, 43 percent of all female rape victims and 9 percent of all male victims were raped by some type of current or former intimate partner. Nearly half (49.3 percent) of all male victims identified by the survey were raped by an acquaintance, compared with 27.3 percent of all female victims (see exhibit 13). About equal proportions of female and male victims were raped by a family member other than a spouse (22.4 and 22.8 percent, respectively). Rapes committed by family members other than spouses tended to occur during childhood or adolescence. Although male victims were more likely than female victims to be raped by an acquaintance or a stranger, it is noteworthy that women are at significantly greater risk than men of being raped by all types of offenders, including acquaintances and strangers.

A comparison of lifetime rape prevalence among men and women by victim-offender relationship shows that 7.7 percent of all women, but only 0.4 percent of all men, were ever raped by a current or former intimate partner; 3.9 percent of all women, but only 0.6 percent of all men, were ever raped by a relative other than a spouse; 4.8 percent of all women, but only 1.4 percent of all men, were ever raped by an acquaintance; and 2.9 percent of all women, but only 0.6 percent of all men, were ever raped by a stranger (see

Exhibit 13. Percentage distribution of female and male victims by victim-perpetrator relationship[a]

exhibit 14). Thus, women are 19.3 times more likely than men to be raped by intimates, 6.5 times more likely to be raped by nonspouse relatives, 3.4 times more likely to be raped by acquaintances, and 4.8 times more likely to be raped by strangers.

As shown in exhibit 15, the victim-perpetrator relationship varies substantially with the age and gender of the victim. Females who were younger than age 12 at the time of the rape tended to be victimized by relatives other than a spouse; female victims who were 12 to 17 years old tended to be raped by intimates and acquaintances; and female

victims who were 18 and older tended to be raped by intimates. In comparison, male victims tended to be raped by acquaintances, regardless of their age at the time of the rape.

Intimate partner rape and termination of relationships

Ending a relationship is commonly believed to pose an increased risk for or escalation of intimate partner violence. This assumption is based on two types of evidence. Divorced or separated women report more intimate partner violence than do married women.[21] Interviews with men

Exhibit 15. **Percentage distribution of child, adolescent, and adult rape victims by victim-perpetrator relationship and victim gender**

Exhibit continued on page 24

Exhibit 15 (cont.) **Percentage distribution of child, adolescent, and adult rape victims by victim-perpetrator relationship and victim gender**

who have killed their wives also indicate that either threats of separation by their partner or actual separation are most often the precipitating events that lead to murder.[22]

To test the theory that the termination of a relationship leads to increased risk of intimate partner violence, study interviewers asked respondents who had been raped by a former spouse or cohabiting partner whether the rape(s) occurred before the relationship ended, after the relationship ended, or both. Exhibit 16 shows that 69.1 percent of the women who were raped by a former spouse or cohabiting partner said they were raped *before* the relationship ended, 24.7 percent said they were raped *before* and *after* the relationship ended, and 6.3 percent said they were raped *only after* the relationship ended. These findings suggest that most rapes perpetrated against women by marital and cohabiting partners occur in the context of an ongoing rather than a terminated relationship.

Exhibit 16. **Percentage distribution of female former intimate partner rape victims by point in relationship when rape(s) occurred (*n* = 288)**

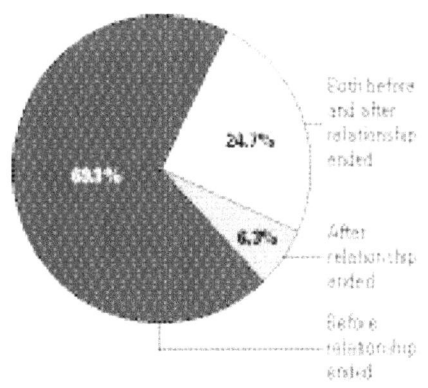

Both before and after relationship ended 24.7%

After relationship ended 6.3%

Before relationship ended 69.1%

Note: Estimates are based on responses from women who were raped by a former spouse/cohabiting partner since age 18. If a woman was raped by more than one former spouse/cohabiting partner since age 18, information about the former spouse/cohabiting partner who raped her most recently was used.

(Too few former intimate partner male rape victims were interviewed to reliably calculate estimates for men.)

It is impossible to discern from the data how many rapes committed against women before the relationship ended were linked to their threats to terminate the relationship. It is also unclear whether women who were raped before and after the relationship experienced an increase in sexual violence at the time of the separation. It is important to note that determining the end of a relationship is a matter of interpretation rather than objective reality. Some of the intimate partner rape victims surveyed may have equated a relationship's end with when they or their partner first discussed termination, whereas others may have equated it with the formal dissolution of a marriage. Clearly, more research is needed on whether terminating a relationship increases the risk of intimate partner violence for women and men.

Characteristics of rape committed against adults

As noted, interviewers asked rape victims detailed questions about the most recent rape suffered at the hands of each type of offender they identified. Because most victims were raped by just one person (see exhibit 6), most were queried about just one rape incident. Characteristics of rapes perpetrated against adult women and men are discussed below. Because the focus is on rapes perpetrated against adults, information presented is based on the most recent rape that occurred since the victim's 18th birthday.

Location of the rape. Survey findings indicate that most rapes committed against adult women and men occur in private rather than public settings (see exhibit 17). Among victims who were raped as adults, 84.5 percent of the women and 64.4 percent of the men said they were

Exhibit 17. **Percentage distribution of female and male rape victims by characteristics of the rape**[a]

Characteristic	Female victims (%)	Male victims (%)
Location of the rape[b]	(n = 717)	(n = 59)
Private setting	84.5	64.4
Public setting	15.5	35.6
Perpetrator was using drugs and/or alcohol	(n = 628)	(n = 53)
Yes	66.6	58.5
No	33.4	41.5
Victim was using drugs and/or alcohol[b]	(n = 726)	(n = 60)
Yes	19.8	38.3
No	80.2	61.7
Perpetrator threatened to harm or kill	(n = 725)	(n = 61)
Yes	31.9	21.3
No	68.1	78.7
Perpetrator committed the following physical assault[c]	(n = 739)	(n = 62)
Slapped or hit	31.4	21.0
Kicked or bit	10.6	11.3
Choked or attempted to drown	13.4	—[d]
Hit with object[b]	6.6	14.5
Beat up	19.4	19.4
Any of the above	37.8	33.9
Perpetrator used a weapon	(n = 733)	(n = 62)
Yes	10.8	8.1
No	89.2	91.9
Victim thought she/he/someone close would be seriously harmed or killed[b]	(n = 726)	(n = 61)
Yes	43.1	21.3
No	56.9	78.7

a. Estimates are based on the most recent victimization since age 18.
b. Difference between female and male victims is statistically significant.
c. Total percentages by gender exceed 100 because some victims suffered multiple types of physical assault.
d. Estimates are not calculated on five or fewer victims.

raped in their home, their perpetrator's home, or some other private setting (e.g., another person's home, a motel room, or a car). Women were significantly more likely than men to be raped in a private setting versus a public setting. This finding undoubtedly reflects the fact that women are more likely than men to be raped by intimate partners.

Alcohol and drug use. Drugs and alcohol play an important role in rape victimization. About two-thirds of the women and men who were raped as adults—66.6 and 58.5 percent, respectively—said their rapist was using drugs and/or alcohol at the time of the rape. In addition, 19.8 percent of the female victims and 38.3 percent of the male victims said they (the victims) were using drugs and/or alcohol at the time of the rape.

Threats, physical assaults, and fear of bodily injury. Compared with male victims, a higher percentage of female victims

reported that their rapist threatened to harm or kill them, physically assaulted them, and used a weapon during their most recent rape as an adult; however, these differences were not statistically significant. An examination of the specific types of physical assaults perpetrated by rapists found that male victims were significantly more likely than female victims to report that their rapist hit them with an object. Why male victims were more likely to sustain this type of physical assault is unknown.

Although female victims and male victims were almost equally likely to be verbally threatened or physically assaulted by their rapist, female victims were significantly more likely to fear their rapist. Nearly half of the female victims (43.1 percent), compared with one-fifth of the male victims (21.3 percent), said that during their most recent rape as an adult they thought they or someone close to them would be seriously harmed or killed.

Injury and Health Outcomes

Injury data indicate that women are nearly twice as likely as men to be physically injured during a rape. Among victims raped since their 18th birthday, 31.5 percent of the women, but only 16.1 percent of the men, said they incurred an injury other than the rape itself during their most recent rape (see exhibit 18). A small number of female victims (3.1 percent), but no male victims, reported contracting a sexually transmitted disease during their most recent rape.

Female victims were also significantly more likely than male victims to report that their most recent rape resulted in penetration (62.2 and 29 percent, respectively). Few male victims said they were penetrated during their most recent rape, a finding that appears to contradict the finding presented earlier that men, like women, are more likely to experience a completed rather than an attempted rape over their lifetime (see exhibit 3). An explanation for this apparent contradiction is not readily available. It is possible that because of the stigma associated with male-to-male sex, male victims felt uncomfortable admitting to interviewers that they had been "penetrated" during their most recent rape.

It also is important to note that findings presented earlier on the lifetime prevalence of attempted versus completed rape are not directly comparable to the findings presented here on the rate of penetration. The earlier estimate refers to the percentage of surveyed men who were victims of a completed versus attempted rape in their lifetime, whereas the estimate presented in exhibit 18 refers to the percentage of male victims who were penetrated during their most recent rape as an adult.

Physical injuries

Most of the female victims who reported being physically injured sustained relatively minor types of injuries, such as scratches, bruises, and welts (see exhibit 19). Relatively few sustained more serious types of injuries, such as broken bones, dislocated joints, sore muscles, sprains, strains, or chipped or broken teeth. (Because only 10 men reported being injured, the study could not reliably estimate the type of injuries or use of medical treatment for male victims.) Of the women who were injured, 36.2 percent said they received medical treatment (see exhibit 18).

Mental health and lost productivity

NVAWS strongly confirms the negative mental health and social costs of rape victimization. Of those raped since age 18, 33 percent of the female rape victims and 24.2 percent of the male victims said they received counseling from a mental health professional as a direct result of their most recent rape (see exhibit 20). The survey found that 19.4 percent of the female victims and 9.7 percent of the male victims raped as adults said their victimization caused them to lose time from work.

Exhibit 18. Percentage distribution of female and male rape victims by injury and health outcomes[a]

Outcome	Female victims (%)	Male victims (%)
Incident resulted in intercourse/penetration[b]	(*n* = 730)	(*n* = 62)
Yes	62.2	29.0
No	37.8	71.0
Victim contracted sexually transmitted disease	(*n* = 732)	(*n* = 61)
Yes	3.1	— [c]
No	96.9	100.0
Victim was physically injured[b]	(*n* = 734)	(*n* = 62)
Yes	31.5	16.1
No	68.5	83.9
Victim received medical treatment[d]	(*n* = 229)	(*n* = 10)
Yes	36.2	— [c]
No	63.8	— [c]

a. Estimates are based on the most recent rape since age 18.
b. Difference between female and male victims is statistically significant.
c. Estimates are not calculated on five or fewer victims.
d. Estimates are based on responses from victims who were injured.

Exhibit 19. Percentage of injured female rape victims who sustained specific injuries (*n* = 231)*

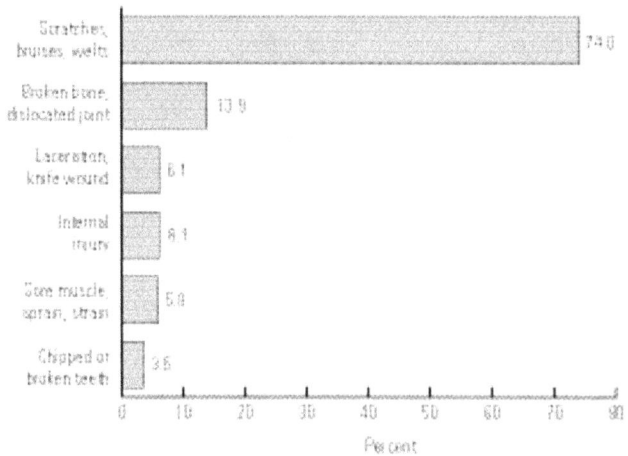

* Estimates are based on the most recent rape since age 18.

Note: Total percentage exceeds 100 because some victims incurred multiple injuries.

Although interviewers did not ask victims about why they lost time from work, it was assumed to be for numerous reasons—to obtain medical treatment, attend court hearings, meet with a psychologist or other mental health professional, and avoid contact with their assailant.

Exhibit 20. **Percentage distribution of female and male rape victims by mental health and lost productivity outcomes***

Outcome	Female victims (%)	Male victims (%)
Victim received counseling from mental health professional	(*n* = 737)	(*n* = 62)
Yes	33.0	24.2
No	67.0	75.8
Victim lost time from		
Work	19.4 (*n* = 736)	9.7 (*n* = 62)
School	7.5 (*n* = 735)	11.3 (*n* = 67)
Household responsibilities	13.0 (*n* = 738)	9.7 (*n* = 62)
Volunteer work	5.7 (*n* = 735)	9.7 (*n* = 62)
Social/recreational activities	23.4 (*n* = 734)	24.6 (*n* = 61)

* Estimates are based on the most recent rape since age 18.

Victims' Involvement in the Justice System

Survey findings confirm previous research that shows rape is a seriously underreported crime. Only 19.1 percent of the women and 12.9 percent of the men who were raped since their 18th birthday said their rape was reported to the police. (See "Total" column in exhibit 21 for estimate on female victims. Estimate for male victims is not shown.) In most (70.2 percent) of the rapes against women reported to the police, the victim rather than a friend, relative, or other third party reported the crime. In the majority of the reports (75.9 percent), the police officer met with the victim and took a report. Only 43.3 percent of the reported rapes resulted in the rapist being arrested or detained. About one-third of the women who reported their rape to the police said the police referred their case to a prosecutor (33.3 percent), referred them to some type of victim service (34.8 percent), or gave them some type of advice (32.6 percent). For those who reported their rape, 9.9 percent said the police did nothing. (So few men reported their victimization to the police that the study was unable to generate reliable information about their subsequent involvement with the justice system.)

When asked why they chose not to report their rape to the police, 21.9 percent of the women who did not report their victimization said they didn't know or refused to answer this question. Those who answered were likely to reply that they feared retaliation from their rapist, were too ashamed of or embarrassed about

what happened to them, or thought the rape was a minor incident or not a police matter (see exhibit 22).

Justice system outcomes

According to victim accounts, 37 percent of the rapes against women that were reported to the police resulted in the rapist being criminally prosecuted. Of the prosecuted rapists, 46.2 percent were convicted of a crime, and 76 percent of the convicted rapists were sentenced to jail or prison (see "Total" column in exhibit 21). Prosecution, conviction, and incarceration rates are substantially lower if they are based on responses from all rape victims, not only those who reported their victimization to the police. Thus, among all women who were raped since age 18, only 7.8 percent said their rapist was criminally prosecuted, 3.3 percent said their rapist was convicted of a crime, and a mere 2.2 percent said their rapist was incarcerated (estimates are not shown in the exhibit).

Thirteen percent of the women who were raped since age 18 said they obtained a restraining order against their rapist (see "Total" column in exhibit 21). Of these women, 65.9 percent said their rapist violated the order.

A comparison of justice system outcomes for women who were raped by a current or former intimate with those who were raped by a nonintimate produced some interesting findings (see exhibit 21).

Exhibit 21. **Percentage distribution of female rape victims by justice system outcomes and whether rapist was intimate or nonintimate[a]**

Outcome	Intimate (%)	Nonintimate (%)	Total
Rape was reported to police	(n = 461)	(n = 273)	(n = 734)
Yes	18.0	20.9	19.1
No	82.0	79.1	80.9
Identity of reporter[b,c]	(n = 84)	(n = 57)	(n = 141)
Victim	78.3	59.6	70.2
Other	21.7	40.4	29.8
Police response[b]	(n = 84)	(n = 57)	(n = 141)
Took report	79.8	73.7	75.9
Arrested/detained perpetrator	46.4	40.4	43.3
Referred case to prosecutor/court[c]	40.5	24.6	33.3
Referred victim to victim services[c]	39.3	29.8	34.8
Gave victim advice[c]	42.9	19.2	32.6
Did nothing	8.3	12.2	9.9
Perpetrator was prosecuted[b]	(n = 81)	(n = 54)	(n = 135)
Yes	32.1	44.4	37.0
No	67.9	55.6	63.0
Perpetrator was convicted[c,d]	(n = 33)	(n = 21)	(n = 54)
Yes	36.4	61.9	46.2
No	63.6	38.1	53.8
Perpetrator was sentenced to jail[e]	(n = 12)	(n = 13)	(n = 25)
Yes	66.7	84.6	76.0
No	33.3	15.4	24.0
Victim obtained restraining order[c]	(n = 452)	(n = 257)	(n = 709)
Yes	17.7	4.7	13.0
No	82.3	95.3	87.0
Perpetrator violated restraining order[f]	(n = 80)	(n = 11)	(n = 91)
Yes	68.8	45.5	65.9
No	31.3	54.5	34.1

a. Estimates are based on the most recent rape since age 18.
b. Estimates are based on responses from victims whose rape was reported to the police.
c. Difference between intimates and nonintimates is statistically significant.
d. Estimates are based on responses from victims whose rapist was prosecuted.
e. Estimates are based on responses from victims whose rapist was convicted.
f. Estimates are based on responses from victims who obtained a restraining order.

Women who were raped by an intimate were almost equally likely as women who were raped by a nonintimate to say their rape was reported to the police (18 and 20.9 percent, respectively). However, women who were raped by an intimate were significantly more likely than women who were raped by a nonintimate to have been the person who reported the rape to the police (78.3 and 59.6 percent, respectively). These findings suggest that women who are raped by a current or former intimate are no more reluctant to become involved with the justice system than women who are raped by nonintimates.

Police were almost equally likely to take a report or make an arrest if the rapist was an intimate or nonintimate. However, they were significantly more likely to refer the case for prosecution, refer the victim to services, and give the victim advice if the rapist was an intimate rather than a nonintimate.

Cases involving intimates were less likely than those involving nonintimates to be prosecuted (32.1 and 44.4 percent, respectively); however, the difference between prosecution rates was not statistically significant. Once they were referred for prosecution, rapists who were intimates were significantly less likely than rapists who were nonintimates to be convicted of a crime (36.4 and 61.9 percent, respectively). These findings indicate that it is more difficult to successfully prosecute rape cases that involve intimates than those that involve nonintimates.

Exhibit 22. **Percentage distribution of female victims who did not report rape to the police by reason for not reporting ($n = 453$)[a,b]**

Reason	Percent
Reported to someone else	1.5
One-time incident, last incident	2.9
Did not want perpetrator arrested	2.9
Did not want police or court involved	3.5
Too young to understand	4.4
Handled it myself	7.7
Perpetrator was husband, family member, friend	8.6
Police would not believe me or would blame me	11.9
Police could not do anything	12.6
Minor incident; not a crime or police matter	17.7
Too ashamed or embarrassed	18.1
Fear of rapist	22.1

a. Estimates are based on the most recent rape since age 18.
b. Total percentages exceed 100 because some victims had multiple responses.

Women who were raped by an intimate were significantly more likely than women who were raped by a nonintimate to obtain a restraining order against their rapist (17.7 and 4.7 percent, respectively). This is not surprising because many State laws that govern restraining orders require the object of the restraining order to be a current or former intimate of the victim.

Satisfaction with the justice system

In general, victims gave the justice system mixed reviews. Of the female rape victims who reported their most recent rape since their 18th birthday to the police, 47.7 percent said they were satisfied with how the police handled their case. This figure increased to 65 percent when only those victims whose rapist was arrested or detained by the police were considered. Similarly, 48.6 percent of the female victims who came in contact with the courts—because their rapist was prosecuted, they obtained a restraining order against their rapist, or both—said they were satisfied with how the courts treated them.

Questions for Future Research

Although NVAWS provides much needed information on the extent, nature, and consequences of rape victimization in the United States, it does not provide all the answers. The survey found that rape prevalence differs among women and men from different racial and ethnic backgrounds. However, how race and ethnicity intersect with other demographic variables was beyond the scope of this study. Research is needed to determine how much of the difference in rape prevalence among men and women from different racial/ethnic backgrounds can be explained by respondents' willingness to report victimization and how much by social, demographic, and environmental factors. For example, future research should examine how age, marital status, and economic stresses such as poverty and unemployment interact with race and ethnicity to increase or decrease the risk of rape victimization.

NVAWS confirms previous findings that show that many rape victims are victimized at an early age, and that women raped before age 18 are twice as likely to report rape victimization as adults. In addition to highlighting the need to direct prevention strategies toward minors, these findings suggest that research should focus on the long-term effects of early rape experiences, especially with respect to the possible causal link between childhood sexual abuse and subsequent sexual abuse.

Future research also should consider the gender and age variations among rape victims and those who commit the crime.

Clearer understanding of how the age and gender of the victim and offender interact with the context and motivations for rape can assist in developing adequate intervention and prevention strategies for rapists and their victims.

More research is needed on risk factors associated with injury, death, and disease incurred during rape victimization of both men and women. Also essential is research on the long-term psychological and social consequences of rape victimization, including depression, posttraumatic stress disorder, lost productivity, and fear of crime.

Despite widespread public education programs, rape remains a largely underreported crime. This finding calls for consideration as to whether law enforcement agencies and victim service providers might expand their efforts to assist rape victims and do more to convince them that reporting their rape to the police is worthwhile and appropriate.

Research of a more qualitative nature is needed to understand the different contexts in which rape occurs, the different ways in which male and female rape victims interpret their victimization, and the processes by which they come to define themselves as rape victims. Qualitative research is also needed on the motivations for rape and the ways rapists minimize and rationalize their aggression.

In addition, cohort and trend analyses are needed to determine whether the

prevalence of rape has increased since World War II and, if so, why? Data from NVAWS show that women under age 50 report significantly more rape victimization than women over 50. Cohort and trend analyses would help determine whether rape prevalence has actually increased or whether younger women are simply more willing than older women to define themselves as rape victims and report their victimization to survey interviewers.

Longitudinal research is needed to determine whether rape victimization early in life increases the risk of rape victimization later in life and, if so, what particular consequences of early victimization make an individual more vulnerable to revictimization. As noted previously, findings establish a clear link between early and subsequent rape victimization for women. However, because NVAWS used a one-time retrospective assessment of respondents' experiences, the data cannot answer certain key questions. For example, did women who were raped as minors suffer some long-term effects (e.g., emotional vulnerability or low self-esteem) that carried over into adulthood and made them more susceptible to being raped as adults? Do certain risk factors for rape in childhood or adolescence (e.g., poverty, sexual orientation[23]) persist into adulthood? Does the relationship between early and subsequent rape victimization uncovered by NVAWS findings reflect the fact that women who were willing to report one type of victimization to survey interviewers (e.g., rape as a child by a family member) were simply more willing to report other types of victimization (e.g., rape as an adult by a spouse), or did recalling early rape victimization trigger recall of subsequent rape victimization?

A longitudinal survey that assessed psychological, behavioral, and environmental characteristics in a representative sample of youths at various times, along with the occurrence of sexual assault victimization between those times, would mitigate some of the problems inherent in a retrospective survey such as NVAWS and help answer such questions. The assumption of a longitudinal design is that if victimized and nonvictimized respondents do not differ at one point in time after controlling for preexisting conditions, but do differ on certain characteristics at a later point in time following a victimization, then those characteristics may be considered outcomes rather than predictors or causes of victimization.[24]

In summary, more research is needed on the characteristics, causes, and consequences of rape and other forms of sexual assault. Future research should focus on the context and motivations for various forms of sexual assault perpetration, risk factors and patterns associated with both sexual assault victimization and perpetration, short- and long-term consequences of victimization, and the relationship between early and subsequent victimization. Studies should incorporate myriad research design strategies, including indepth interviews with victims and perpetrators, longitudinal surveys of both youth and adult populations, and police and court record reviews.

Notes

1. National Research Council, *Understanding Violence Against Women,* ed. Nancy A. Crowell and Ann W. Burgess, Washington, DC: National Academy Press, 1996: 9–10.

2. For example, rape victimization estimates generated from the Bureau of Justice Statistics' National Crime Victimization Survey are substantially lower than rape victimization estimates generated from the National Women's Study (see National Victim Center and Crime Victims Research and Treatment Center, *Rape in America: A Report to the Nation,* Arlington, VA: National Victim Center and Charleston, SC: Crime Victims Research and Treatment Center, 1992).

3. National Research Council, *Understanding Violence Against Women,* 40–44 (see note 1).

4. Ibid.

5. NVAWS was conducted from November 1995 to May 1996. Respondents reported on events that spanned the 12 months prior to their interview. Thus, a person who was interviewed in November 1995 reported on events that occurred between November 1994 and November 1995; a person who was interviewed in May 1996 reported on events that occurred between May 1995 and May 1996.

6. Michael, R.T., J.H. Gagnon, E.O. Laumann, and G. Kolata, *Sex in America: A Definitive Survey,* New York: Warner Books, 1994: 223.

7. National Victim Center and Crime Victims Research and Treatment Center, *Rape in America* (see note 2).

8. Special tabulation was done by Bureau of Justice Statistics staff using 1995 National Crime Victimization Survey data, September 2001.

9. See, for example, Tjaden, Patricia, and Nancy Thoennes, *Full Report of the Prevalence, Incidence, and Consequences of Violence Against Women: Findings From the National Violence Against Women Survey,* Research Report, Washington, DC: U.S. Department of Justice, National Institute of Justice, and U.S. Department of Health and Human Services, Centers for Disease Control and Prevention, November 2000, NCJ 183781.

10. The two rape screening questions used in NCVS are as follows: (1) (Other than any incidents already mentioned,) has anyone attacked or threatened you in any of these ways . . . (e) Any rape, attempted rape, or other type of sexual attack? (2) (Other than any incidents already mentioned,) have you been forced or coerced to engage in unwanted sexual activity by – (a) Someone you didn't know before – (b) A casual acquaintance – OR (c) Someone you know well?

11. See, for example, Helton, A.M., "The Pregnant Battered Women," *Responses to Victimization of Women and Children,* 9 (1) 1986: 22–23; and Koss, Mary P., "Detecting the Scope of Rape: A Review of Prevalence Research Methods," *Journal of Interpersonal Violence,* 8 (2) (June 1993): 198–222.

12. Greenfeld, L.A., and S.K. Smith, *American Indians and Crime,* Washington, DC: U.S. Department of Justice, Bureau of Justice Statistics, February 1999, NCJ 173386.

13. Wallace, L.J.D., A.D. Calhoun, K.E. Powell, J. O'Neil, and S.P. James, *Homicide and Suicide Among Native Americans, 1979–1992,* Violence Surveillance Summary Series, No. 2, Atlanta, GA: U.S. Department of Health and Human Services, National Center for Injury Prevention and Control, 1996.

14. Bachman, R., *Death and Violence on the Reservation: Homicide, Family Violence, and Suicide in American Indian Populations,* Westport, CT: Auburn House, 1992.

15. See, for example, Sorenson, S.B., J.A. Stein, J.M. Siegel, J.M. Golding, and M.A. Burnam, "The Prevalence of Adult Sexual Assault: The Los Angeles Epidemiologic Catchment Area Project," *American Journal of Epidemiology,* 126 (6) (1987): 1154–1164; and Sorenson, S.B., and C.A. Telles, "Self-Reports of Spousal Violence in a Mexican American and a non-Hispanic White Population," *Violence and Victims,* 6 (1991): 3–16.

16. National Research Council, *Understanding Violence Against Women:* 40–41 (see note 1).

17. Bergen, R.K., *Wife Rape: Understanding the Response of Survivors and Service Providers,* Thousand Oaks, CA: Sage Publications, 1996.

18. Tjaden, Patricia, Nancy Thoennes, and Christine J. Allison, "Comparing Stalking Victimization From Legal and Victim Perspectives," *Violence and Victims,* 15 (1) (2000): 7–22.

19. The National Women's Study (see note 2) found that 29 percent of all forcible rapes of females occurred when the victim was younger than 11 years old, and another 32 percent occurred when the victim was between ages 11 and 17.

20. See, for example, Browne, A., and D. Finkelhor, "Initial and Long-Term Effects: A Review of the Research," in *A Sourcebook on Child Sexual Abuse*, ed. D. Finkelhor, Beverly Hills, CA: Sage Publications, 1986: 156; Coid, Jeremy, Ann Petruckevitch, Gene Feder, Wai-Shan Chung, Jo Richardson, and Stirling Moorey, "Relation Between Childhood Sexual and Physical Abuse and Risk of Revictimization in Women: A Cross-sectional Survey," *The Lancet*, 358 (9280) (August 11, 2001): 450–454; Messman-Moore, Terri L., Patricia J. Long, and Nicole J. Siegfried, "The Revictimization of Child Sexual Abuse Survivors: An Examination of the Adjustment of College Women With Child Sexual Abuse, Adult Sexual Assault, and Adult Physical Abuse," *Child Maltreatment*, 5 (1) (2000): 18–27; Miller, J., D. Moeller, A. Kaufman, P. Divasto, P. Fitzsimmons, D. Pather, and J. Christy, "Recidivism Among Sexual Assault Victims," *American Journal of Psychiatry*, 135 (1978): 1103–1104; and Russell, D.E.H., *The Secret Trauma: Incest in the Lives of Girls and Women*, New York: Basic Books, 1986.

21. Klaus, P., and M. Rand, *Family Violence*, Special Report, Washington, DC: U.S. Department of Justice, Bureau of Justice Statistics, 1984, NCJ 93449; Stark, E., and A. Flitcraft, "Violence Among Intimates: An *Epidemiological Review*," in *Handbook of Family Violence*, ed. V.B. Van Hasselt, R.L. Morrison, A.S.

Bellack, and M. Hersen, New York: Plenum Press, 1988: 307–308; and Zawitz, M.W., *Violence Between Intimates*, Washington, DC: U.S. Department of Justice, Bureau of Justice Statistics, 1994, NCJ 149259.

22. Bernard, M.L., and J.L. Bernard, "Violent Intimacy: The Family as a Model for Love Relationships," *Family Relations*, 32 (1983): 283–286; and Daly, M., and M. Wilson, "Evolutionary Social Psychology and Family Homicide," *Science*, 242 (1988): 519–524.

23. Duncan, D.F., "Prevalence of Sexual Assault Victimization Among Heterosexual and Gay/Lesbian University Students," *Psychological Reports*, 66 (1990): 65–66, and Tjaden, Patricia, Nancy Thoennes, and Christine J. Allison, "Comparing Violence Over the Life Span in Samples of Same-Sex and Opposite-Sex Cohabitants," *Violence and Victims*, 14 (4) (1999): 413–425.

24. White, Jacquelyn W., and John A. Humphrey, "A Longitudinal Approach to the Study of Sexual Assault: Theoretical and Methodological Considerations," in *Researching Sexual Violence Against Women: Methodological and Personal Perspectives*, ed. Martin D. Schwartz, Thousand Oaks, CA: Sage Publications, 1997: 22–42.

OTHER PUBLICATIONS FROM THE NATIONAL VIOLENCE AGAINST WOMEN SURVEY

The following NIJ publications provide more information about the National Violence Against Women Survey (NVAWS):

- *Stalking in America: Findings From the National Violence Against Women Survey*, Research in Brief, by Patricia Tjaden and Nancy Thoennes, Washington, DC: U.S. Department of Justice, National Institute of Justice, and U.S. Department of Health and Human Services, Centers for Disease Control and Prevention, April 1998, NCJ 169592.

- *Prevalence, Incidence, and Consequences of Violence Against Women: Findings From the National Violence Against Women Survey*, Research in Brief, by Patricia Tjaden and Nancy Thoennes, Washington, DC: U.S. Department of Justice, National Institute of Justice, and U.S. Department of Health and Human Services, Centers for Disease Control and Prevention, November 1998, NCJ 172837.

- *Extent, Nature, and Consequences of Intimate Partner Violence: Findings From the National Violence Against Women Survey*, Research Report, by Patricia Tjaden and Nancy Thoennes, Washington, DC: U.S. Department of Justice, National Institute of Justice, and U.S. Department of Health and Human Services, Centers for Disease Control and Prevention, July 2000, NCJ 181867.

- *Full Report of the Prevalence, Incidence, and Consequences of Violence Against Women: Findings From the National Violence Against Women Survey*, Research Report, by Patricia Tjaden and Nancy Thoennes, Washington, DC: U.S. Department of Justice, National Institute of Justice, and U.S. Department of Health and Human Services, Centers for Disease Control and Prevention, November 2000, NCJ 183781.

To obtain copies of these publications, visit NIJ's Web site at www.ojp.usdoj.gov/nij; contact the National Criminal Justice Reference Service at P.O. Box 6000, Rockville, MD 20849–6000, 800–851–3420 or 301–519–5500; or send an e-mail message to askncjrs@ncjrs.org.

The following journal articles, book chapters, and other documents have been published about NVAWS:

- Patricia Tjaden and Nancy Thoennes, "Prevalence and Incidence of Violence Against Women: Findings From the National Violence Against Women Survey," *The Criminologist*, 24 (3) (May/June 1999): 1, 4, 13–14.

- Patricia Tjaden, Nancy Thoennes, and Christine J. Allison, "Comparing Violence Over the Life Span in Samples of Same-Sex and Opposite-Sex Cohabitants," *Violence and Victims*, 14 (4) (1999): 413–425.

- Patricia Tjaden and Nancy Thoennes, "Prevalence and Consequences of Male-to-Female and Female-to-Male Intimate Partner Violence as Measured by the National Violence Against Women Survey," *Violence Against Women*, 6 (2) (2000): 142–161.

- Patricia Tjaden and Nancy Thoennes, "Stalking in America: Prevalence, Characteristics, and Police Response," in *Problem-Oriented Policing: Crime-Specific Problems, Critical Issues, and Making POP Work*, vol. 3, ed. Corina Solé Brito and Eugenia E. Gratto, Washington, DC: Police Executive Research Forum, 2000: 113–138.

- Patricia Tjaden, Nancy Thoennes, and Christine J. Allison, "Comparing Stalking Victimization From Legal and Victim Perspectives," *Violence and Victims*, 15 (1) (2000): 7–22.

- Patricia Tjaden, "Extent and Nature of Intimate Partner Violence as Measured by the National Violence Against Women Survey," Symposium on Integrating Responses to Domestic Violence, *Loyola Law Review*, 47 (1) (2001): 41–57.

- Patricia Tjaden and Nancy Thoennes, "Coworker Violence and Gender: Findings From the National Violence Against Women Survey," *American Journal of Preventive Medicine*, 20 (2) (2001): 85–89.

- Patricia Tjaden and Nancy Thoennes, "The Prevalence of Rape by Clergy and Other Types of Perpetrators," *The Resource*, Fall/Winter (2002): 3.

- Patricia Tjaden, Nancy Thoennes, and Christine J. Allison, "Comparing Stalking Victimization From Legal and Victim Perspectives," in *Stalking: Perspectives on Victims and Perpetrators*, ed. Keith E. Davis, Irene Hanson Frieze, and Roland D. Maiuro, New York: Springer Publishing Company, 2002: 9–30.

- National Center for Injury Prevention and Control, *Costs of Intimate Partner Violence Against Women in the United States*, Atlanta, GA: U.S. Department of Health and Human Services, Centers for Disease Control and Prevention, March 2003.

- Patricia Tjaden, "Prevalence and Characteristics of Stalking," in *Stalking: Psychology, Risk Factors, Intervention, and Law*, ed. Mary P. Brewster, Kingston, NJ: Civic Research Institute, 2003: 1–19.

To learn more about CDC prevention activities related to family violence and intimate partner violence, visit CDC's National Center for Injury Prevention and Control Web site at www.cdc.gov/ncipc/dvp/dvp.htm.

To learn more about NIJ's violence against women research portfolio, visit NIJ at www.ojp.usdoj.gov/nij/vawprog/welcome.html.

About the National Institute of Justice

NIJ is the research, development, and evaluation agency of the U.S. Department of Justice. NIJ's mission is to advance scientific research, development, and evaluation to enhance the administration of justice and public safety. NIJ's principal authorities are derived from the Omnibus Crime Control and Safe Streets Act of 1968, as amended (see 42 U.S.C. §§ 3721–3723).

The NIJ Director is appointed by the President and confirmed by the Senate. The Director establishes the Institute's objectives, guided by the priorities of the Office of Justice Programs, the U.S. Department of Justice, and the needs of the field. The Institute actively solicits the views of criminal justice and other professionals and researchers to inform its search for the knowledge and tools to guide policy and practice.

Strategic Goals

NIJ has seven strategic goals grouped into three categories:

Creating relevant knowledge and tools

1. Partner with State and local practitioners and policymakers to identify social science research and technology needs.
2. Create scientific, relevant, and reliable knowledge—with a particular emphasis on terrorism, violent crime, drugs and crime, cost-effectiveness, and community-based efforts—to enhance the administration of justice and public safety.
3. Develop affordable and effective tools and technologies to enhance the administration of justice and public safety.

Dissemination

4. Disseminate relevant knowledge and information to practitioners and policymakers in an understandable, timely, and concise manner.
5. Act as an honest broker to identify the information, tools, and technologies that respond to the needs of stakeholders.

Agency management

6. Practice fairness and openness in the research and development process.
7. Ensure professionalism, excellence, accountability, cost-effectiveness, and integrity in the management and conduct of NIJ activities and programs.

Program Areas

In addressing these strategic challenges, the Institute is involved in the following program areas: crime control and prevention, including policing; drugs and crime; justice systems and offender behavior, including corrections; violence and victimization; communications and information technologies; critical incident response; investigative and forensic sciences, including DNA; less-than-lethal technologies; officer protection; education and training technologies; testing and standards; technology assistance to law enforcement and corrections agencies; field testing of promising programs; and international crime control.

In addition to sponsoring research and development and technology assistance, NIJ evaluates programs, policies, and technologies. NIJ communicates its research and evaluation findings through conferences and print and electronic media.

To find out more about the National Institute of Justice, please visit:

http://www.ojp.usdoj.gov/nij

or contact:

National Criminal Justice
 Reference Service
P.O. Box 6000
Rockville, MD 20849–6000
800–851–3420
e-mail: *askncjrs@ncjrs.org*